Jump

A poetry book
by Brandon Cohen

Acknowledgments

I would like to thank everyone who encouraged me throughout the years and especially the people who have poems written about them in this collection.

Additionally, I would like to thank and give a shoutout to Jenna Dresel for the cover art. Jenna is a fantastic artist who captured my vague idea and turned it into something beautiful.

Finally, I would like to thank you for reading this. No matter what happens from here it's incredible to me that I could write something people care to read, and no one can take that away from me. Hopefully you can find something in here that makes you feel something.

Collections

Jump- A collection of poems about love.

Burn- A collection of poems about the tragedy of losing that love.

Radiate- A collection of poems about rising through adversity.

Shrink- A collection of poems about the adversity we go through in order to exist.

Introduction

If God is reading this

I hope he enjoys

Introduction II

If the Devil is reading this

I hope he enjoys

Introduction III

If you are reading this
I hope you enjoy

Jump

Unique

She had five eyes

Four noses

Three chins

And everybody laughed at her

So she gave up an eye

A nose

A chin

But everybody still laughed at her

So she gave up everything that made her her

Until she looked like everybody else

And nobody cared to notice her

Unique II

"Normalcy is a disease"
My Grandpa used to teach me
But when I tried to fake sick
With a case of being normal
My teacher simply laughed
I guess I should have learned a lesson

Lucky

I tripped on a crack

Fell onto your lap

Now I don't believe in superstitions

Impressions

"You certainly know how to make a first impression"
I didn't know what I was doing at all
But it was the best thing I've ever done

Maternal Instincts

She shivers, wrinkling her nose up at the stars
Wondering aloud if they're cold
Above the stars, the sun peers down
Hoping we're not too cold

Those Who Wait

They say good things come to

I never knew

Because I could never wait to find out who

Blue Eyes

You said I have the bluest eyes

As I swam a lap in yours

Drowned myself in yours

Lost myself in yours

Forgetting how to see

Anything but yours

Mona Lisa

Please stay still
For just this moment
So I can paint myself a memory
That can live forever

Wanderlust

My Grandma used to say "happiness is a pebbled
path"
I never knew what that meant
Until I met you

When You Meet Her

When you meet her you will feel a wave of calm crash over you like a tsunami, tearing down the hopelessness inside and replacing it with splashes of sunlight and reminders of loveliness. You will not reach for your life vest to pull you above the surface, you will submerge deeper into the flooding, finding comfort.

You will realize butterflies can breathe underwater too, circling the whirlpool she has created in your gut with an excitement matching your own as a child on the first day of summer.

When you meet her you will understand why stars elect to remain above. The sun returns home nightly and whispers about the beauty she has seen, convincing the sprinkles in the sky not to fall out of fear of turning a dull shade of envy.

You will realize clouds are couches for souls that wish to live vicariously through you, having floated along, never meeting their mates. You will catch snowflakes on your fingers and watch daydreams of former loves play out until they melt away with a silent direction to follow.

When you meet her you will finally understand why the girl you insisted was the girl of your dreams in High School dumped you before college. She was not the girl of your dreams, she was one too many drinks on a Saturday night, thinking that love is found in the bottom of a bottle of Bud Light.

You will realize the girl of your dreams is in front of you, but it is a different kind of drunk. If a cop asked, you could not recite the alphabet backwards, forwards, sideways, upside down. You could not even name a letter. Asked to walk in a straight line, you would walk like a child playing don't step on the lava, dancing around to meet her eyes. If the cop asked your address, you would say cloud and he would shake his head and let you off the hook with a warning; cupid is on the loose.

When you meet her you will remember your Grandpa telling you that love feels like home. She will tear down the walls of uncertainty inside, painting murals of hands merging in bags of popcorn at the movies, drunken lips colliding on repeat, a quartet of words you wrote in the sand that leaves her lips paralyzed, but her head nodding in delight. Her eyes will be the only TV channel you wish to tune into, the sound of her car door closing and the click-clack of her heels inching towards the "welcome home" mat will sound like Beethoven's symphony. You will regret laughing as a child when your Grandpa advised you to remember the ancient proverb, "Home is where the heart lives." You will understand he was wise, as you look upon your castle of cherish.

There are 615,000 results for "I feel like my heart skipped a beat" on Google. When you meet her, you will realize why.

Cliches

It's the day dreams, the songs she sings, the wave of calm her aura brings, keeping my mind from floating to the trouble things. A blanket ever-lasting on my shoulders keeping me warm, butterflies in my stomach in a constant swarm, the last drop of rain in a thunderstorm. Cliches lining the page, all about you, rhymes that can't capture all that you do. But I will always try.

Thesaurus

I wanted to describe how beautiful you are
But couldn't find the words
So I bought a thesaurus
And you are so alluring, appealing, charming, cute,
dazzling, delicate, delightful, elegant, exquisite,
fascinating, fine, gorgeous, graceful, grand, lovely,
magnificent, marvelous, pleasing, pretty, splendid,
stunning, superb, wonderful.

I Wish To Be

I wish to be so many things. I wish to be the sunlight that awakens you in the morning. I wish to be a blanket on a snowy evening covering you from the cold. I wish to be a melody that plays over the dark thoughts that fill your brain. I wish to be a walking reminder that loneliness is no more than a persuasive stranger, and love is all around you. I wish to be a dictionary of self-help definitions. Remember, you exist. I'm so happy you exist. I wish to be the joke that makes you laugh so hard that milk shoots out of your nose. I wish to be the butterflies in your stomach when someone compliments you the right way. The way you deserve. I wish to be the crunching of the autumn leaves, the foliage that fills your eyes with magnificent colors. I wish to be the smell of a new book, the excitement to turn the page and get to the next chapter. To keep going. I wish to be the way you feel on Christmas, presents scattered underneath the tree. Knowing that people know you. Knowing that people care. I wish to be your flashlight in the darkest of places. I wish to be less cliche for you. I wish to be a safe haven from the storms that come and go. I wish to be the sun, the sky, the stars, and the moon. I wish to be everything for you.

Jump

They asked if I would jump off a bridge if you did first

Truth is I would jump first

To test the water, to make sure it isn't too cold

To ensure you land safely

To serve as a trampoline, lifting you back up

To fall for you one last time

Even if you change your mind

Slip Into The Void With Me

You loathe the summer sun
She burns your sensitive skin
I complain about the winter winds
As they mock the mess we're in

Your daddy issues go on display
Every time you date
So when I drunk call about my Mother
You believe in fate

Despite shaky hands and blackened minds
We can always see the light
So I guess we're teaching one another
Two wrongs must make a right

They say misery loves company
So let's take a table for two
We can laugh away our demons
Until they're laughing too

Rainbow

Roses are red
Violets are blue
I could not find a more cliche way
To say how I appreciate you

Roses are red
Violets are blue
I saw in black and white
Until I met you

Roses are red
Violets are blue
Now I embrace my colors
And hope to shine like you

Grey Skies

We huddled beneath the awning
As the rain cried down
The sky was airing its grievances
Yet I couldn't hide my smile
Winds roared at my trembling legs
But it was you who blew me away

Maps

I used to fear losing my way
I forged the same path every day
Until one time I saw a face
Made me change my entire pace
Now no clue where to go
Only fear, but this I know
There is so much beauty in your blues
I'd learn the way just for you

The Church of You

I spent 18 years attending church

Listening to Gospels

But the smile you slip between our lips greeting

Is what leads me to believe

Blonde

Fall on my shoulders

In a warm embrace

Find comfort on my pillow

On my jacket

Anywhere and everywhere

Until I brisk you away

Always hoping for more

If I Leave You On Read

Odds are I've been swallowed by the moon

Swept up by the stars

Stunned by the sights and sounds

Or by the warmth of her lips

The glow of her eyes

The soothing hum of her voice

I will not be asleep

I will be the next day's sunrise

Skeleton

My hands tremble
My bones are brittle
My skin is thin
But when you embrace me
There is no body I would rather call home

Safety Net

Though I am slender and shaky

You must understand

I can be your steady hands

Chorus

My heart sings the loveliest song when I see you
I hope you can hear it too

Home

It was a quarter past far too late
And I asked you to take me home
So we didn't move an inch

To Be Continued I

Appreciate the good times

The next wave won't wait

I hope you've found a poem you like

Before it gets too late

If you wish to venture ahead, go forth

But I must tell you this

The poems ahead speak of broken hearts

Not a lover's kiss

Burn

Stung

I stopped to smell the roses
And got stung by a bee

Chicago

How strange it was to learn
That you could be in my arms
Fitting together so perfectly
Yet even in that moment
You felt miles away

Disenchanting

After our first date I wrote you a poem
And you said you loved it
And you showed it to all of your friends

After our third date I wrote you a poem
And you said you loved it
And you shared it online

After I asked you to be mine I wrote you a poem
And you said you loved it
And you showed it to your Mom and Dad

After our first fight I wrote you a poem
And you said you appreciated it
And you kept it to yourself

After I didn't see you for the holidays I wrote you a
poem
And you said it was nice of me to do that
And you never told me what you did with it

Last week I wrote you a poem

And you said you would get around to it

And you never read it at all

Thesaurus II

I threw away my thesaurus
I don't want to describe you anymore

The Sun

The sun is no different than you or I

She wishes to embrace

But if she gets too close

Everyone burns

Rotten

Often it feels
I am pulling your weeds
From my skin
So I can be my own garden
And finally grow

Suffocation

I love you

Do you love me?

I love that you love me

Do you still love me?

I love that

Is everything okay?

Okay

I wish you still loved me

Summer

Blooming flowers wilt beneath your feet
Your boots crushed the last of them
I picked you a dandelion to make you smile
And the wind blew it away

Unspoken Farewell

You sneak softly into the night
Footsteps failing to make a sound
I awake to find you gone
Beginning diverging paths

Yet as you forge your own way
I do not seek re-connection
I do not wonder
I remain

A Storm Brews

I bottle my anger and send it to Sea

Only to see it hurled back

"I am not a home for untold rage,"

She cries

"Don't you ever wonder how storms begin?"

Accident

You are the mud stuck to the sole of my shoe

I am a U-turn into heavy traffic

You are dragging me through uneven sidewalks

I am spinning out of control

Tick Tock

Tick tock

The clock is running laps and I cannot keep up

Tick tock

My throat is on fire with words unspoken

Tick tock

I'm sorry it took me two drinks

Tick tock

To spill two years

Tick tock

But when we were golden

Tick tock

I swear time stood still

Tick tock

And I long to linger on your lips once more

Tick tock

But our time has passed

Wicker

One day under neon lights
Drunk on wine and in a haze
We will find each other smoking cigarettes
Neither of us smoke but it will feel like fate
With warning signs fixed across our foreheads
But maybe your lips will smell like strawberry
And mine bubblegum
Almost enough

Perhaps the past will sit as a shadow
Holding a boombox above its head
Incredibly cliche
Incredibly us
But slowly
Like a candle gasping for one last breath
Together
We will melt

Whisper

Whisper my name
In between smoky breaths
Your lips emit
It's winter

Whisper my name
Into my ear
Like it's gospel
Like it's spring

Whisper my name
A firefly's song
That lost its tempo
At the end of summer

Whisper my name
So I can remember
What once lingered
Before the fall

Parasite

I offered you a piece of me
And you took and you took and you took
From all I was

So I re-grew as a parasite
And I took and I took and I took
From everyone else

So I crawled through seeping skin
And I bit and I ticked and I stole
Until there was no one left

So I saw only the creature in the mirror
And I stopped and I shifted and I reanimated
Until I was a butterfly

And now harmless I roam free

Who Am I?

I am
Detaching from my skin
Hollowed out like a shell
on sand

I am
Accepting apologies
That never escaped your
lips

I am
Stars
Seeing stardust in self-
inflicted wounds

I am
A flower
On the tombstone of who
you made me be

I am
Questions
Can I do it? Can I make it
through?

I am
Answers
I can do it. I am enough.

I am
The tattoo on the lower
lip of your back
Belonging to you

I am
Begging you to stay
While showing you the
door

I am
More myself than I will
ever be you
My own flesh and blood

I am
Leaving you behind
For the flowered road
ahead

Hearing Things

Tonight I swear I heard your voice
A faint whisper between gusts of wind
"Are you okay?"
I felt tireless

Tonight I saw the sun rattling her cage
But the dull, grey gate budged not
Drops of snowflaked tears fell from the sky
I felt cold

Tonight I heard winter roaring in laughter
Reminiscing tales of nights spent alone
Tales of nights inside my head
I felt weak

Tonight I learned to sleep without song
Tonight I shined, myself a light
Tonight I am existing everywhere
Tonight I am strong

A Suicide Note

His lips where mine belong

Inferno

What do I think of?
Burning buildings
I saw

In your eyes
Looking down
When I made you blush

Does he notice?
You laugh like a child
When you're high

Atop burning building
Looking down
On me

Trying to sleep
With vacancy
Wondering

If you are a ghost

And I am a ghost

Can we see each other?

Fragments

There is nothing left

                                        You stole

Every piece of me

                                        I loved
The way you peeled from my lips to sneak a smile
Thinking I wouldn't notice

                                        I noticed
There is nothing left

                                        You stole

Every memory of you

                                        I dreaded

The way you peeled them from my skin
Until into torn up polaroids

                                        I fell apart

Momentos

How strange it is

To sit in a shoebox beneath your bed

As you lie stoic in a picture frame

Beneath old poems I never got to read to you

Not Us, Not Us, Not Us

Not us, not us, not us. How could we fall apart?. We were invincible. We were a tidal wave crashing over anyone that dared to doubt us. We were weeknights spent lying under the covers, ignoring the thunderbolts being thrown between my mother and father beneath us. I didn't realize love could be sunlight until I met you. We were Friday nights in the fall spent jumping in leaves, laughing as if we were kids again. Saturday nights spent floating around parties, mixing love and liquor into a perfect haze. Sunday nights spent with my Grandpa, listening to his tales of past love and how forever could be real, trust him, he knows from experience. Forever could be us. I never felt warmer than when he would speak and you would listen.

Listen, you said. You never started sentences like that, you were always bubbling with concepts and smiles, so when your voice dropped an octave and your eyes looked dull, I knew something was off. You told me things had changed, you were seeing things differently and I wasn't in your field of view.

Through all the streetlights and star-brights, the neon signs on stores we used to hold hands in, I saw memories, you could only see a dead end now.

Now the memories slip through the cracks in my head like sand through an hourglass, I can no longer remember whether you were drinking milk or water when i made you laugh so hard your nose flooded I can no longer remember your brother's favorite movie that I watched with him only to get closer to you.

Your aunt, the one with the purple hair, Alice, right? No maybe Annette. Right, Annette. That has to be it. When she met me, she told me to enjoy it while it lasted. I never understood why she would say something like that at a dinner party. I wanted to know what happened to her to make her that cold to a stranger filled with nothing but love and maybe a little bit of wine.

Now I understand she was a highway sign, flashing "DANGER AHEAD" but I was too busy looking at the passenger seat to listen.

Now we drive under the sky, our souls vacant beneath the black and blue.

Black and blue, the colors discovered when your Father's fist met my eye. I expected a handshake, but when he saw my clothes on your floor and my lips on your neck he wanted to unglue me the only way he knew how. He never gave me a second chance, but please tell him I'm sorry for the mess I left behind for him. I wish I could have been around longer to help. I remember the battle that waged between you two when he found out you were still dating me a few months later. World War 3 has already happened, and it sounds like your Father's bombastic instruction telling you not me, mixed with your cries, "you can't do this to us! Not us. Not us. Not us." Not us. You were right, he couldn't do it to us. We were invincible, remember? I wrote a story the other night out of the blue. The words arrived in my head like they had been sitting in a queue, waiting to flow onto the pages. The story is about a girl who thought she was unlovable, she was more familiar with teardrops and shot glasses than arms around her or expressions of admiration. The story is about a boy who used to be able to speak novels to that girl, the same one that looked at him like he was the answer to a question that was always lingering in her mind. Now he speaks in short stories, always getting cut off before the good part of the story.

The story starts with a beginning, he's drawn in by her vibrant eyes at a party, and rushes over with a line to win her affection. He trips over his words and trips over a crack in the sidewalk, spilling them all over her until her dress is soaked and he's told her everything he's seen. She gives him a kiss on the cheek and he has to look down at his shoes because he feels he must be melting. They spend the night laying on a field underneath the stars, as cliche as can be, but they don't care. On her lips he can taste stardust. In her eyes he can see the moonlight. They entangle on top of the world.

The climax is my favorite part, the boy and the girl are a modern day Romeo and Juliet. In her ears, he whispers "I look for you in everyone," In his ears, she whispers "I'm always thinking about you." In her dreams she sees him as a cowboy, lassoing away her demons with a smile, "not today boys." Together, they like to skip rocks and say they're only a stone's throw away, knowing they will never feel alone.

Together they must be invincible.

The end is where I struggle. No one ever told me that Romeo and Juliet die in the end. No one ever told me that forever for one is not forever for another, or that looking to the passenger seat and seeing an imprint leftover from the night she said goodbye would finally cause him to melt. She says she doesn't really think about him anymore. Her demons are on the loose, She says she's been having night terrors, she's seeing someone new now, Insomnia. Insomnia knows the boy only as a great threat, so Insomnia sneakily slips stones into the pockets of the relationship. then sends it to the lake.

I wrote this story the other night and my editor returned it with a picture of us splashed across the cover. "The story of us" he wants me to call it.

Please tell me it's not an autobiography. We were invincible, remember? We were invincible. Come back to me, I know you're there. Come back to me, these bones are too fragile to carry the weight of missing you.

Come back to me, I want to tear the pages of this story out and set them on fire, but my lighter is still in your bedroom drawer. Come back to me, we can make a bonfire out of it together and laugh until enough tears come out to extinguish the flame. Remember, like we used to? Come back to me, please don't let this story be about us. Not us, not us, not us.

To Be Continued II....

Before it gets worse

There is a calming wave

I hope this makes you smile

Radiate

This Little Light of Mine

We are not our mothers, we are not our fathers

We are not mistakes, their mistakes

They made decisions, selfish decisions

A house is not always a home

A parent is not inherently golden

I will radiate despite her

Millennials

The future is a tattoo parents never approved
The future is a protest sign peeking out of the
huddled masses
The future skipped class to attend a lecture on
feminism
The future bought earplugs for Thanksgiving dinner
The future hears your statement, but raises you a
question
It's what you taught us, show your work
The future will not stop until the question has been
answered
The future will not be patronized
Your experiences are not universal
The future is terrified of what you've done
But the future is determined
The future will be okay

High

Father's screams blast louder than blaring stereos

Mother's pacing moves like the beat

Hazy eyes cannot fall in rhythm

Because a bag of Cheetos sounds like your favorite

song

Marathon

He asked me to run a mile in his shoes

So I slipped on his raggedy life

Seeing questions hale from the sky

Feeling a weight drop on my shoulders

Dragging me down

As I readied myself to run through the storm

I finally understood

Blooming

There's a garden outside my grandfather's apartment
With flowers hopelessly clinging to life
When I arrive with a can they cannot muster any
tears
Nor whisper a thank you
But I know they will be okay

The colors drain and the leaves wither as they are left
Dark like the sky when the sun leaves to sleep
Yet the sun rises again and hope holds her hand
And I know the flowers will refresh and grow again
Everything will be okay

Supernova

They told me of a star

That exploded into a light so bright

It was nearly an entire galaxy

I hope that's how I go

Begin Again

Maybe memories you once thought infinite are as fleeting as the moon at dawn, maybe nostalgia is the only lover that will stay the night, maybe your hands tremble at the thought of trying to identify yourself in this never ending maze. That's okay. The clock always strikes midnight. Every day is a new life.

Simplicity

I hope you learn the innocence of a child
The imagination of the naive
The creativity of an open book
One that needs a story

I hope you learn simplicity
No impossibilities
No impracticalities
Only poetry in motion

Mixtape

I will learn every song on every instrument

If it will get you out of bed

I will write you self help song books

If it would make a difference at all

I will embrace the calluses on my hands

If that's what it takes to kickdrum your heartbeat

I will be the mixtape you play on a rainy day

And I will never skip a beat

Decisions

Twinkle twinkle little star
Show me where the good things are
Point me in the way to go
Just this once I'd love to know

When my compass turns to dust
When I can't, but I must
Twinkle twinkle little star
Show me where the good things are

To The Girl On The Suicide Hotline

I told myself I was calling you because I had nothing
better to do.
I told myself I was calling you because the last
episode of Rocket Power was over, and a phone call
with a stranger sure as hell beat an episode of Ren &
Stimpy.
I told myself I was calling you because maybe *you*
needed someone to talk to.
I told myself a lot of things.
Maybe that's why I called you.

To the girl on the suicide hotline,
I'm sorry I never got your name.
It's just when I started to speak my mouth drooled
out waves of depression I never knew existed.
Suppressed memories cascaded into conversation like
they had been sitting in a queue.

My lungs emitted every word I locked away from my therapist.
I'm sorry I forgot to ask how you found the key.

To the girl on the suicide hotline,
Thank you for listening to my mixtape of grievances.
I cried all the words that lingered.
"I'm tired of performing autopsies for lost friendships."
"I'm tired of attending funerals of relationships that died without leaving notes."
"I'm tired of mourning living people."
You asked how long I'd been tired and I couldn't catch my breath to answer.
I expected you to disappear into thin air, a magic trick so many performed before.

To the girl on the suicide hotline,
When you began rattling off possible solutions to me, my hockey senses tingled.
I was a defenseman, combatting each method of self-help you shared.

But you were a freight train of help coming and I an ant on the tracks.

You spoke of writing as a saving grace, of my brother's smile I must have slipped into the pocket of conversation when depression wasn't looking, of the way my grandfather lit up when Frank Sinatra's voice filled the airwaves. You spoke until I caught my breath.

To the girl on the suicide hotline,
I never knew that CPR could be performed through spoken words.
I never knew that empathy could stitch together open wounds.
I never knew that a stranger would introduce me to hope.
We've been steady for three years now.
I can't believe it's been three years now.

To the girl on the suicide hotline,
I'm sorry I hung up before thanking you.
I'm sorry I hung up before learning your name.

But it's just like you said,

I had a lot to get out of bed for.

I have a lot to get out of bed for.

Shrink

A Christmas Story

It's Christmas and you're celebrating
With your Father
Who left your Mother
When he found out what she did
He still sings carols all the same

It's Christmas and you're celebrating
With your friend
Who sees herself the devil
While her halo faintly flickers
Opening fits with excitement

It's Christmas and you're celebrating
With strangers
Making small talk in shallow voices
Their stories linger in the winter air
As they wear their holiday spirit disguises

It's Christmas and you're celebrating
With anyone at all

That there's 7 billion people living different plots

And everyone is alone

So no one is on their own

Father?

Answer my call
When I am desperate
Abandon me
When I am not

Write your list of demands
On the back of a funeral program
For children
Gone too soon

　forbid I slip
　forbid i sin
Or I must get on my knees
Or I must bare my soul

I wonder where hypocrisy falls
Among the devilish deeds
I wonder where I fall
For being a stranger

But the word says you love

And it's proclaimed you forgive

So tell me dear

Why must I ache so?

Truths and Lies in Troubled Times

Pour it down your throat like a bottle of bleach, swirl it around until you choke on it. It's a bitter pill you can't stand to swallow, but hey, the lump in your throat has been lonely lately. Cover your self-inflicted wounds with bandages, tell your friends what the devil on your shoulder whispered in your ear when they ask why you're bleeding. Wonder where the angel went. Make sure to check in with regret on an hourly basis, she worries you'll do something smart. Circle back with your insecurities, they know you'll do what they want. "How do you feel?" used to be such an easy question, but with your throat slammed shut all you can do is fake a smile.

Re-Done

I am no more than piled up bodies
Corpses of my former selves
Discarded attempts at existence

You held no funerals
You mourned no losses
You cried no tears

I used to be my own self
But don't you worry
You taught me better than that

Validation

You take it from a friend
Leaving them with no choice
But to medicate your self-doubt
But to blindly give

The mirror stares, frowning
At the freckle you named Judas
The one who steals
The one who makes you beg

Perhaps you're cowered in a corner
At a party
At a concert
In the bathroom of a local bar

You see swaying arms and smiling faces
Making it look so easy
It's never felt half as easy
You plead for it to be easy

One day it will be yours

Like a love that kickdrums your heart

Like a song that snugs across your eardrums

Like the feeling when you give it to someone else

Mixtape II

Take my favorite song

Forget its name

Mess up the lyrics

Sing it out of key

Like what you've done to me

Toy Story

Talk me down into your playsize toy
Dress me down in spewed criticisms
"Can't you do anything right?"
Leave me alone, naked

Make sure to place me down abruptly
With force
Rattle my bones
With disgust

You know you can
You know I'll be sitting there when you return
You promise me you'll be back soon
Just like old times

First you break the promise
Then you break me
Leaving me to piece myself back together
Until you're ready to play once more

Prayer

A child's legs knelt on a pew
Starting conversation with distant stranger
Told his response would not come through word
He waited

A boy's legs quivered under a desk
Like on a cold night, like under a weight far too heavy
Once told his response would not come through word
He waited

A man's skin smeared scarlet
As a desperate plea for attention
Once told his response would come not through word
He waited

At the bar sits a man who has not been heard
His voice shrunk into a whisper
No longer willing to wait for a response, he pleads
"When do I get to be happy?"

Labels

Your best friend's words leave you squeamish
She laughs at the weight you bear
You laugh along
Choking on your confessions
Shrinking into a shadow, black and white
Caution tape shielding your colors

Clipped Wings

I am no more than a flustered bird
Fluttering about
On my good days I fly
To the highest highs
Immersed in the bluest skies
But when skies are grey
And I have a bad day
My wings hesitate
And fault
So all I do is fall

White and Blue

He sits in a crowded basement
Sweat cascading down his neck
Hostile eyes strangling common sense
He sees a reflection of his younger self
His nose is bloody too

When he was a child he cried at needles
Until his Father stroked his hair
"It's going to be alright, son"
Now he thinks his Father a liar
And doesn't shed a tear

Vacancy

I am grasping at painted wrists
Like lotto tickets
All scratched up

You are grabbing the wheel
As I swerve around potholes
You swear do not exist

We are stuck in black and white
Colorblind
Trying to stay alive

Unwelcome

His hands find my shoulders
I shrink into a child once more

Snakes

Do not bite the hand that feeds you

It may be poisoned

Do not grasp for familiar hands

They may be calloused, they may be cold

Anxiety

SometimesIfeelliketheworldismovingtooquicklyforme
andeveryonearoundmeismovingattheirowncomfortab
lepacefloatinglikenothingcanhurtthemlikenothinghas
everhurtthembeforebutIamspeedingfrompointAtopoi
ntBtryingnottobelatetryingnottolooktoorattledtryingn
ottoletanyonedownwhenallIwanttodois B R E A T H E
butIneverlearnedhowtoslowdownIneverlearnedhowt
oletthingssimplybehowtoletmyselfbewhoIwantobeeve
nifthatmeanssomethings s l o w i n g d o w n
formyownsakeforthesakeofmysanityforthesakeofmyli
feforthesakeofmywritingandIknowIneedto r e l a x
andrememberthatIamonlyhumanIamonlyonepersonI
amdoingthebestIcanandthatiswhatcountssoasIthinka
boutthatIcanfinally learn to slow down to the right
pace and be me.

Mumble

You said you could barely hear me and that didn't surprise me at all because I lost my voice when I was a child and never found a way to get it back.

Dissociate

I am somewhere inside myself

Wandering yet again

I am searching for myself

Wondering yet again

Where I go

Bittersweet

Like a goodbye you never saw coming

Like an embrace that took you by surprise

Like your first love getting married

Like your next love meeting your eyes

Like a song you can't quite get out of your head

Like a song you never want to leave your head

A strange, familiar feeling

Bittersweet

High II

Your brain is filled with dirt

You forgot my birthday

You baked me a cake of spiders

I didn't know what to say

Your brother pulled me to the side

Said "hey dude, I like this vibe but I don't like you"

You were somewhere in the stars

I didn't know how to pull you down

Your brother was over the moon

I didn't know if I should pull him down

I never liked needles much

But I sure liked you

Atrophy

Your skin and eyes held a competition
To see which could paint themselves grayer
And they both won
So everybody lost

Ribs

They gave you your rib in a glass jar

As a token

For being broken

You kept it on your nightstand

So every time she would come over

She was reminded

She never had all of you

Your Ex-Lover Is Alive

I saw your Father sitting by an oak tree
Crouched over
Picking at dead flowers alone

I saw your Mother at the liquor store
Preparing for a party
We both know she'll drink too much at

I saw your sister at the restaurant
She was a hostess
But she still wouldn't meet my eyes

I swear I saw you in the clouds
I went to text you
And remembered I could not anymore

Let Me Tell You About My Best Friend

The first time I saw you, you were so, so stoned, sipping on a glass of whiskey, telling me how wonderful sobriety could be. You always spoke in contradictions, explaining the beauty of what you would not do for yourself. When I told you I was scared, you said you didn't know the feeling.

I remember the time you climbed down the neighbor's fence and pierced your forearm along the way. As the blood slowly swam down your wrist, you laughed about how you were as high as the stars and couldn't feel it anyway. Every time I stopped speaking, you asked me if I lost my voice. You always did the talking anyway.

I remember the time we went to the concert and you jumped right into the middle of the mosh pit. Intoxicated by the moment and several shots of your favorite beer, you blended in like you had been there for the entire night. You said the room was spinning like your favorite record and you didn't want the moment to stop.

The last time I saw you, we were quietly gazing up at the stars. You were high above the milky way, eyes redder than the blood that still sits stained on my neighbor's fence. You spoke quietly, saying you were scared. I heard the words, but I didn't understand what they meant until I couldn't tell which star was yours.

When I saw you inanimate for the first time, your Father patted me on the shoulder. He asked me how I was feeling, so I said I was scared. He told me he knew the feeling all too well.

Thank You For Reading

If you read these poems
Or even just one
I hope you are okay
If you read none at all
I hope you are okay
You are not alone
You will never be alone
Thank you for reading

About the Author

I started writing poetry when I attended Hofstra University during my sophomore year of college. I took a Creative Writing course taught by Professor Robert Plath which changed my understanding of writing and how enjoyable it could be.

In the ensuing four years I would write poems whenever they came to mind, often about what was happening in my life, but sometimes about subjects that I felt inspired to attempt to capture.

The first poem I wrote in this collection was When You Meet Her, and at no point did I write a poem for the sake of writing a poem.

I could not tell you what's coming next for me, but I'm excited to see what it is. Thank you for reading!

www.ingramcontent.com/pod-product-compliance
Lightning Source LLC
Chambersburg PA
CBHW070518030426
42337CB00016B/2012